A fresh collection of
Jeffrey & Janice's
funniest moments

Young
at **Heart**

A STUDIO PRESS BOOK

First published in the UK in 2020 by Studio Press,
an imprint of Bonnier Books UK,
The Plaza, 535 King's Road, London SW10 0SZ
Owned by Bonnier Books,
Sveavägen 56, Stockholm, Sweden

www.studiopressbooks.co.uk
www.bonnierbooks.co.uk

© Thea Musselwhite 2020

1 3 5 7 9 10 8 6 4 2

ISBN 978-1-78741-852-3

Text and photography by Thea Musselwhite
www.boldandbright.co.uk

Edited by Sophie Blackman
Designed by Rob Ward

A CIP catalogue for this book is available from the British Library

Printed and bound in Poland

A fresh collection of
Jeffrey & Janice's
funniest moments

Young
at Heart

STUDIO
PRESS

He was in shape for his age.
Unfortunately that shape
was a potato.

Love is...
letting the other one
know when you're
going for a poo.

The crows have called.
They want their feet back.

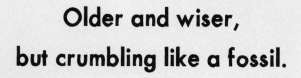

**Older and wiser,
but crumbling like a fossil.**

**Another year closer
to that mid-life crisis.**

You're never too old
to get drunk and
do stupid sh*t.

Welcome to retirement.
You may not know what you're
doing with your life, but at
least you are also
very poor.

Remember, laughter is the best medicine... unless you've got the sh*ts.

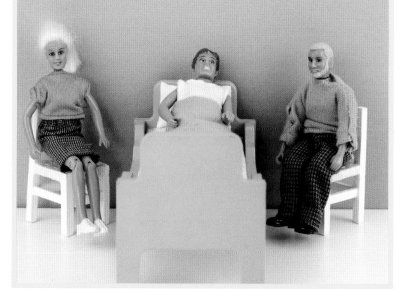

You used to
climb mountains,
but now you need to
steady yourself to fart.

**Finally old enough
to do what I want...
too tired to actually
do it.**

The birthday suit was beginning
to look like it could do with
a good iron.

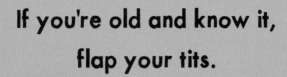

**If you're old and know it,
flap your tits.**

Like a fine cheese,
he was getting
stinkier and squishier
with age.

Your mind thinks you're 29.
Your sense of humour suggests
you're 14. Your body is asking
why you're not dead yet.

Hitting the "unsubscribe"
button to adulthood,
but still f*cking here.

Old enough to
remember the hardships
of life before Google.

He reminded them that because he wiped their arses, one day they'd have to do the same for him.

He chuckled to himself
as he drove off in his
children's inheritance.

I want to grow
old and disgusting
with you.

He was getting on a bit,
but he still had a
tremendous cock.

**Feeling like a tired,
old bastard?**

There's a nap for that.

She needed a moisturiser to hide the fact that she'd been tired since 1989.

If she were a pigeon, she knew who she would sh*t on.

**Life is better
when you're an old fart.**

Now that they'd started swinging with the neighbours, no one minded the odd overhanging bush.

She didn't want to sleep like a baby (those little f*ckers never sleep). She wanted to sleep like a husband.

Ageing well: Cheese and wine
Ageing badly: You and bananas

One year closer
to crazy cat lady
that stinks of wee.

He hadn't lost all of them, but there was definitely a hole in the bag.

They say you are what you eat, but he didn't remember eating a sexy beast.

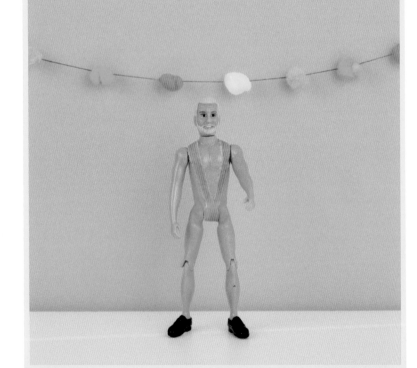

Even though she was getting on a bit, she still had a mighty fine ass.

**Now they were older
they needed a support bar
in the bathroom.**

Work medium, play medium

(we're not as young as we used to be).

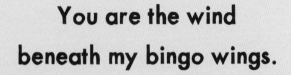

You are the wind
beneath my bingo wings.

Old enough to know better.
Young enough to
do it anyway.

He was about:
20% stud
80% muffin.

Her Christmas list was short:

Don't wait until your deathbed
to tell people how you feel.

Tell them to f*ck off now.

When I said I wanted to be a hot chick, menopause was not what I had in mind.

He danced like no one was watching. They weren't. They were busy looking at sh*t on the Internet.

If you're overly competitive about being more tired than someone else then marriage might be for you.

His body was not a temple.
It was a crumbling old relic
that was probably haunted.

In dog years...
still old as f*ck.

Emotional baggage is easier to carry when it comes with love handles.

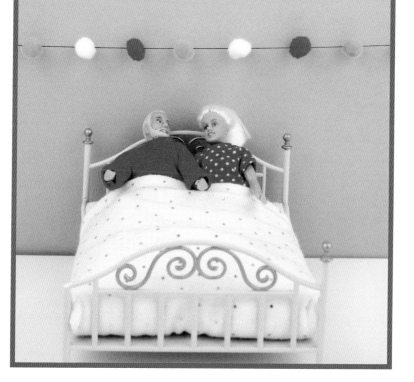

The neighbours had asked if
they'd like to go dogging.
They had no idea what that was.
Thank goodness for Google.

He was no spring chicken...
he was a wrinkly old cock.

The best bit about retirement?

Doing f*ck all.

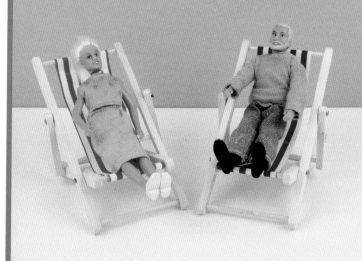

Life's all fun and games
until your metabolism
slows down.

**Hobbies are important
when you retire.
Their hobby was wine.**

If you can't say something nice, say it to your other half... they're not listening anyway.

**They were both
born to be wild...
until about 9 p.m. or so.**

She Googled her symptoms and it turned out that she just needed everyone to f*ck off.

Once he shaved his balls he got three seconds off his best time.